Colour Cotton Therapy

This book is dedicated to returning to the *Essence*

Published by Yelfor Pty Ltd

c/- Post Office UKI NSW 2484 Australia
  www.colourcottontherapy.com

National Library of Australia
Cataloguing-in-Publication data:

Morning Clouds.
Colour Cotton Therapy.

Includes index

ISBN 0 9757452 0 4

1. Mind and body therapies. 2. Colour-Therapeutic use. 1. Title.

128.2

Sincere appreciation to Beryl Bender Birch for the use of the quotation on page 19 from her book Beyond Power Yoga.

Photographers: Ken Ball, Colin Cooksey, Atredes and Clayton Lloyd

Graphic design, colour seperations, prepress: Clayton Lloyd / Flawless Imaging
www.flawlessimaging.com

Printed in China by Everbest Printing Co.

Disclaimer

The energy work of these colours is to assist a person in bringing about a change within themselves and restoring equilibrium.

I am not dispensing medical advice, diagnosis or prescriptions. I make no claims, recommendations or representations confirming any physical, mental or emotional effects in using the contents of this book to treat, alleviate, prevent or cure a persons health.

Whenever any person finds themselves in need of treatment by a medical practitioner, I encourage them to seek a duly licensed practitioner and or to continue medical treatment and or seek independent medical advice.

Both the author and publisher disclaim any liability as a result of the use or application of any of the contents of this book. Persons using this book do so entirely of their own choice.

Please note:
If you are not a medical practitioner, do not contravene any of your State or National Laws by diagnosing or prescribing.

Morning Clouds

Acknowledgements

This book acknowledges my love and gratitude to:

Swain, my beloved partner,

Thel, my first born, and Wood, my apprentice.

In loving memory of

Les Elphick for gifting me the existence of these Cottons.

Gratitude also is acknowledged for a number of reasons to the following people, to whom I would like to say thank you.

Jackie Fitzgerald my first teacher, Enid Bailey, Kay Andrews, Vicky Christiansen and to the late Cam Dawson, for his wizardry.

A special thanks to Michael Breen for his suggestion for me to create this Introductory Book, David Ackerman, M. Chiro B.Sc., Kevin Masman, the geomancer of Masman Envirosurveys and Ken Ball for cloud inspiration.

Aurigae, my scribe, and Chloé Dauphin, the messenger.

Love to you all, Morning Clouds

Origins

by Morning Clouds

Morning Clouds is an innovative and inspirational person, and a pioneer for new thought in the context of her surroundings.

Originally from Melbourne, with her partner, she managed the conversion and running of a large Bio-dynamic dairy farm, where the healing modalities of Reiki, Kinesiology and Homeopathy were used on the land and on the animals.

Being drawn to go to New Zealand, she was gifted the Colour Cottons by Les Elphick, who at the age of nineteen, was cured of a terminal illness using Colour Cottons. In this work, Morning Clouds recognised a powerful healing tool. She has recreated this work into a book, to make its form more elegant, more refined and simplified, so that the true essence of the energies may be experienced. Colour Cotton Therapy, (CCT) only existed as a broad body of knowledge prior to this transformation.

This new body of work has been achieved by drawing other healing modalities into play, to optimise the coloured cottons use. It is now offered to you freely, that it might inspire and awaken a true heart response.

Contents

Introduction to colour cotton therapy

These colours are a unique form of vibrational healing that relate to the body, the subtle energy system and their specific frequencies. These frequencies implode into the cellular system, then explode through every cell nucleus. The resonance of colour energy vibrations in this book can enable one to feel their wholeness and experience emotions such as compassion and to feel great joy. Perhaps more pointedly, to connect the user with their own power to bring balance and harmony to the body-mind.

The cottons have evolved by matching the wavelength of our negative cellular structures with the right colour, and infused with the right geometry of mathematics. By joining these cottons together, creates a circle that has no beginning and no end. They are crossed, then folded into the shape of the Infinity sign, resembling a rose, opening the heart from which healing and love flow. The pulsating geometry of thought-form gives out a vibration strengthening the body to resist disease and to heal itself. These energies may also stress the dis-ease causing organisms, so that they no longer survive, helping the body to release karma and pain.

Almost since the moment of your birth, you have been taught either by your parents, teachers or friends into using your logic and reasoning. We create our own reality. We also come to transcend certain lessons and karma.

One of my own personal lessons that I created in my life as a young girl occurred when I noticed that our garage was on fire. I ran in to tell my father, but he did not believe me. I then went out again to recheck what I had seen, and that it was the truth. This incident created a fear or a doubt of not being believed.

Fear reaction of whatever degree reflects a lack of self-confidence. All our fears begin in conscious thought. Fear is exhausting and contracting. Fear can be the basis of all emotions such as anger, sorrow and jealousy. You are these emotions. Go beyond this. Release the fear. C.C.T. can support and help you to be stronger, for you are the creative energy in your life. You have the imagination, the healing capabilities and the desires. But you are more than this. You have the capacity to be love itself. It is your rightful possession.

We must be responsible for each and every thought that we put out. No one can coerce you, or demand change or insist on attitudinal change. This can only come from within. Some resistance may be encountered, even sabotage of some kind. This is due to fear. By being willing to release fear, the desired change will be achieved quickly and effectively.

In using this colour therapy work, harmonisation within the body may be felt virtually instantly, or it may manifest over time. When a shift occurs, you may notice changes within yourself, or others may notice it.

Our body can be compared to an onion. It has many layers (emotions); these layers can be peeled one by one, or you can go straight to the core (source). There is always a negative emotional response behind a dis-ease state. With all negative emotions and experiences this becomes a wound. We then place a wall around this as a defence mechanism to protect us from the hurt or pain. We create a mask when we don't feel safe or so that we do not have to face a negative emotion.

As you begin working on yourself, it will become self-evident that other issues will arise. As Zachary Ziamus quoted "underneath the rigid rocks of fear, usually lie the treasure of opportunity".

My feeling is that our aura is like a tapestry. The colours are a record of an individual's thoughts, emotions or experiences, past, present and future. Breathing reflects the emotions. Feel the breath. Notice the body's reactions to the different emotions.

When we change our breathing, the emotions change. Feel into all reactions. But whatever thoughts or feelings arise about what you are doing or have done, feel what you are presently experiencing, and feel the breath of life. Tears are a way of expressing your emotions.

Move deeply into the feelings that are occurring. Allow yourself to be vulnerable. Feel the breath, relax, and continue to be the silent witness of your thoughts.

The stimulating vibrations of these colours can be the catalyst in raising a person to a higher state of consciousness; lifting us to a place where they can consciously or unconsciously bring balance, empowering the body's own resources to achieve harmony and well-being.

You made a promise to yourself. That promise was to rediscover the truth, the truth that has been locked away, awaiting its return. It has been there all this time, that deep knowingness, being able to surrender into happiness. That moment could be right now to awaken you to know that all you are is love. Living in perpetual darkness has robbed you of witnessing this truth. Remember, the mind is the door; the heart is the lock; the key being the discipline of attention.

The energy in this body of work unlock the heart, allowing new changes to take place, acknowledging the body to be a body of Light, as we feel the Truth of our existence.

How to use CCT

Colour is everywhere, but its essence is not seen. These colour energies are a transformational experience. They are tools that can be used to restore harmony to the body-mind. CCT draws out our soul qualities and they become a potent force in our transformation.

Choosing an Intention:

To choose the appropriate colour, focus mentally on the colour frequency your body needs. Or if it helps, write it down. You need to clarify the issue, problem or direction that is required, such as:

- To dissolve a particular issue you are dealing with.
- Guidance or protection
- To attain higher vibrations in meditation
- Achieving a greater sense of inner balance and harmony
- Releasing old karmic patterns or tendencies held in the body-mind.

Selection Method

There are a variety of methods that can be used to select the appropriate colour. Kinesiology, intuition, sensation, dowsing, or pendulum can be used, but the easiest method is by opening the book at random and choosing the colour that you are drawn to in relation to your intent.

Subtle Energy Body

Human consciousness expresses itself in physical form through different energy fields. These fields can generally be classified as the Chakras, Meridians and Auric fields.

Each of the energy fields has an optimal frequency for health and overall well-being.

A disturbance of consciousness, left unresolved, results in a deviation from this optimum frequency.

Therefore, it is beneficial to restore the optimal harmonic frequency of these energy fields, which can also bring about a resolution of disturbance of consciousness. Naturally this requires awareness.

All of the various energy systems, chakras, and meridian energy fields, have their own unique connections. Therefore, through their relatedness, they express the totality of consciousness as a unified field.

In order for this energy balancing work to go much deeper and be more effective and lasting, it is highly recommended to have a clear space for this to be carried out.

Using the colours

Find a quiet comfortable place to sit and relax. Take two or three long deep breaths to center yourself and to connect to your Higher Self. Remember, the more you relax, the more receptive you are to receive the vibration that is required. Be totally conscious and fully present.

Place your middle and index fingers on the colour chosen. With eyes closed, and again taking a deep breath, allow this vibration to be assimilated by the body. Continue receiving the energy vibrations for as long as required until you feel that the healing is complete. You may even enhance this by visualising the colour chosen or by focusing the colour on a particular area of your body. With practice you can learn to intuit the areas of the body that need attention. If your thoughts are drifting, bring your awareness back to the vibrations.

You may experience some sensations, such as a sudden clarity of mind or even a release of energy where there was once a blockage. These can be experienced as heat, coldness, tingling, perspiration, throbbing, heaviness and pulsing or even numbness. You may also not necessarily experience any sensations. Just observe what is happening in the body, without reaction or judgement, just observe with awareness.

As you proceed observing the feeling, you are learning to witness the reality of how your body feels. This practice is done diligently with the wisdom of what is arising in the body. The truth is observed within the bodily sensations. There is no imagination involved, rather direct full awareness, with recognition.

You may also feel whether another frequency is required at this time to complete the process. (Try placing under your pillow whilst sleeping!).

Remember to take time every day to relax and play, have a laugh and learn to listen with awareness to your body, to regain optimum health, harmony and happiness.

We are like shining suns,

and our obstacles are like passing clouds.

The clouds obscure the light,

and we forget the sun is shining.

So we actually believe that it is cloudy.

But our practice helps us to remember that

the sun shines brightly behind the clouds.

Aura

....mirrors the flow of life

The body and mind are manifestations of cosmic energy vibrating at both gross and subtle frequencies. The physical body is the most dense* of these fields. Underlying both is the subtle energy body, also known as the electromagnetic field or auric field that can be seen existing around the physical body. This aura can be seen by people who have intuitive vision, and also through Kirlian photography.

This energy phenomenon can be considered to be a bio-plasmic field that interpenetrates, arising from the collective contribution of emotions and energies within the body. This plasma/aura is composed of both positive and negative charged ions.

The aura is quite variable in its appearance because it represents a spectrum or a flowing together of what is surfacing in the consciousness from moment to moment.

*Lowest vibratory current

Aura

....lifeforce

Chakras

....deals with physical

A chakra is an energy centre that corresponds to certain aspects of consciousness within a human being. Each chakra expresses both energetic and conscious qualities, as well as having a direct link to the nervous system.

Bringing the chakras back into optimal harmonic frequency can have a profound effect in creating unity within the mind-body and heart. It also allows for a deeper understanding and experience of one's being, by bringing awareness of the underlying cause of the disturbance within the chakra field.

This occurs because the physical body correlates with each chakra and in turn, affects the central nervous system.

In order to have optimal health, alignment and integration of the chakras must occur, both within each chakra and the system as a whole.

Base Chakra

....existence

Sacral Chakra

....joy

Solar Plexus

....guidance

Heart Chakra

....belong

Throat Chakra

....expression

Brow Chakra

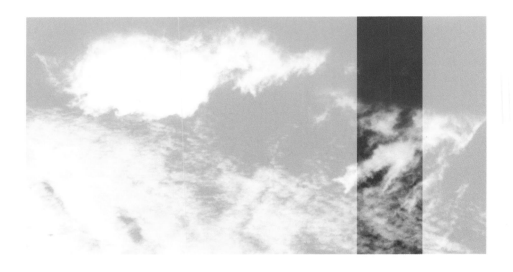

....awakening

Crown Chakra

....becoming

Meridians

....interconnects organs

The meridians are pathways for the flow of energy within the body. There are fourteen major meridians, and each meridian is associated with both an organ and an emotion. When the emotion associated with a particular meridian arises strongly within an individual, this can result in a vibratory imbalance of that meridian.

It is relevant to note that there are other factors influencing the healthy function/frequency of each meridian such as food, seasons, time of day or temperature.

The meridians serve as the energetic framework of the physical body and so have a strong influence on the healthy function of the spine and central nervous system.

Excluding the Central and Governing Meridians, which exist in the mid line of the body, the other twelve meridians are located on both sides of the body forming their energetic or electrical circuits.

Central Meridian

....flow

Governing Meridian

....guide

Stomach Meridian

....surrender

Spleen Meridian

.....understanding

Heart Meridian

....freedom

Small Intestine Meridian

....closure

Bladder Meridian

....clearing

Kidney Meridian

.....*honesty*

Circulation / Sex Meridian

....enjoyment

Triple Warmer Meridian

....exposure

Gall Bladder Meridian

....acceptance

Liver Meridian

....vitality

Lung Meridian

....revealed

Large Intestine Meridian

....truth

Glands

....alignment and refinement

The glandular or hormonal system works in conjunction with the nervous system in the expression of consciousness.

In this way, different hormones are seen as the medium of both emotion and energy in the body.

Although they are most definitely a physical occurrence, their influence extends far beyond the physical realm, since they can affect the mental, psychic or even subtler realms of our consciousness.

A strong connection exists between the various glands and chakras, and this occurs because some of the chakras have glands of the endocrine system as their physical basis.

Pituitary Gland

....organiser

Pituitary Gland

...director

Pituitary Gland

....releaser

Pineal Gland

....light body

Thyroid Gland

....interplay

Thyroid Gland

....respect

Thymus Gland

....constitution

Thymus Gland

.....cleaning

Adrenal Gland

....to shift

Pancreas

....allowing

Testes

....propagation

Testes

....strength

Ovaries

....embraced

Ovaries

....to release

Underground Water

....motion and movement

A symphony of subtle energies comprises the hidden geomantic landscape. When these energies are in balance and in harmony they will support our physical, mental and spiritual well being. When out of harmony they undermine our well being.

Water flows in underground fissures and fractures, and projects an energy field to the surface to which dowsers respond.

This field may carry information. Such information may be one of pollution, if the water is chemically polluted, flow tension, if its channel is restricted, or it maybe a wonderful source of life promoting vitality.

Tension may exist between two underground streams that cross (looking from above).

Underground Water

....undercurrent

Electromagnetic

....disruptive intensity

Electromagnetic Radiation (EMR) is literally everywhere, and is emitted by mains powered electrical appliances, transformers, switches, hand and hair dryers, electric shavers, microwaves, electrical lighting, cellular phones, computers, radio and television transmitters, relay towers and orbiting satellites, plus much more.

The electromagnetic spectrum spans a wide range of frequencies and wavelengths of energy, which is transferred (or radiated) in a wave pattern.

This form of radiation can result in a number of health defects, both on the physical and mental levels.

Electromagnetic

....infiltrating

Electromagnetic

....saturated

Electromagnetic

....deflecting

Mercury

....corrosion and accumulator

Mercury has been included in this book, because being a heavy metal it is not normally found in the human body.

It is recognised that the body absorbs mercury from amalgam fillings, causing mercury poisoning. This inorganic mercury is characterised by causing a wide range of conditions affecting many organs and having a detrimental effect on the immune system.

Even when these fillings are removed, the mercury still has to be removed from the tissues within the body.

Systemic toxicity is produced by inhalation of mercury vapour, especially when mercury-silver fillings are removed, resulting in absorption of these highly toxic fumes.

Consult a specialist dentist as to the appropriate measures of carefully removing amalgam fillings.

Please note: mercury can also be found in some fish.

Mercury

....villainous

Feng Shui

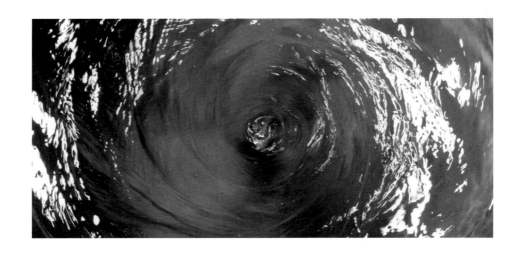

....this will open hearts

Chinese traditional wisdom believes there are five main factors that govern our quality of life.

Destiny - the set of energies we carry through life and their inevitable expression over time governs our potential.

Luck - our capacity to utilise, manifest and maximise our gifts as given by our destiny. This is something we cannot manipulate.

Feng Shui - environmental influence of all kinds.

Virtues - the qualities we develop to get on with others in a harmonious way. Especially our capacity to give of our energy, time and support to others.

Education / Work - our skills and capacity and willingness to work towards our goals.

Touch this vibration colour regularly, allowing the energy to start with conscious thought, infusing the entire house with light and energy, clearing your whole environment.

Feng Shui

....enter a new beginning